BUILD FABULOUS
FIGURES

ILLUSTRATED BY SEBASTIAN QUIGLEY

DK

www.dk.com

London • New York • Stuttgart • Sydney

BALLERINA

It takes hours of practice for a ballerina to learn to hold this pose.

YOU WILL NEED

1 each of these pieces

2 each of these pieces

4 each of these pieces

This beautiful ballerina is now ready to practise her pirouettes!

There are **27** bricks in this ballerina model.

6

5

4

3

2

1

These bricks will make her hair.

START with the ballerina's head.

IDEAS
• Change the colour of the ballerina's tutu – she'll need a new costume for every ballet she dances.
• Make two horizontal legs for the ballerina – then she will do the splits!

8

Attach the head to the body.

7

Add these two yellow bricks for the hands.

4

3

2

1

Now make the ballerina's body – don't forget her tutu!

6

5

4

3

2

1

Now build her legs. Remember to attach the two white ballet shoes.

BUILD this model from the base brick upwards.

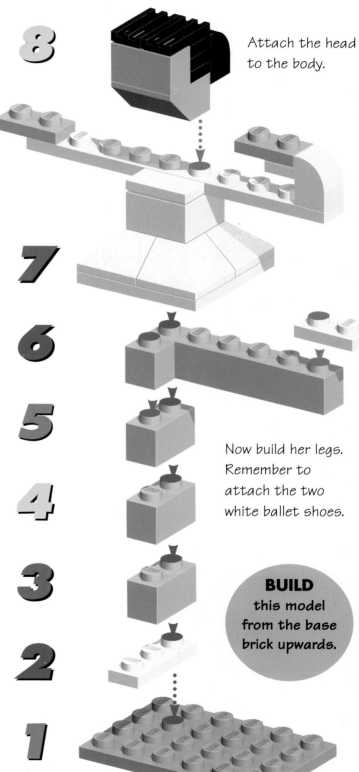

BODY BUILDER

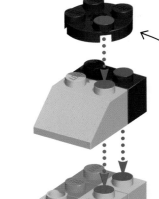

This big body builder will be one of your strongest models!

YOU WILL NEED

1 each of these pieces

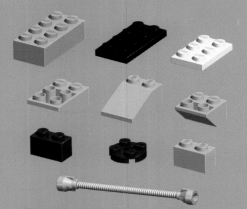

2 each of these pieces

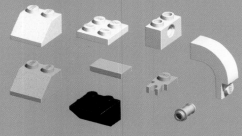

4 of this piece

There are **32** bricks in this body builder model.

8

7

Now give your model some hair.

6

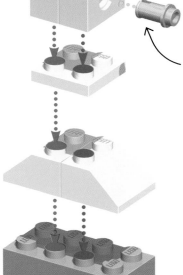

5

4

Remember to attach these bricks! The arms will fit on later.

3

2

1

START with the body and carefully build in layers.

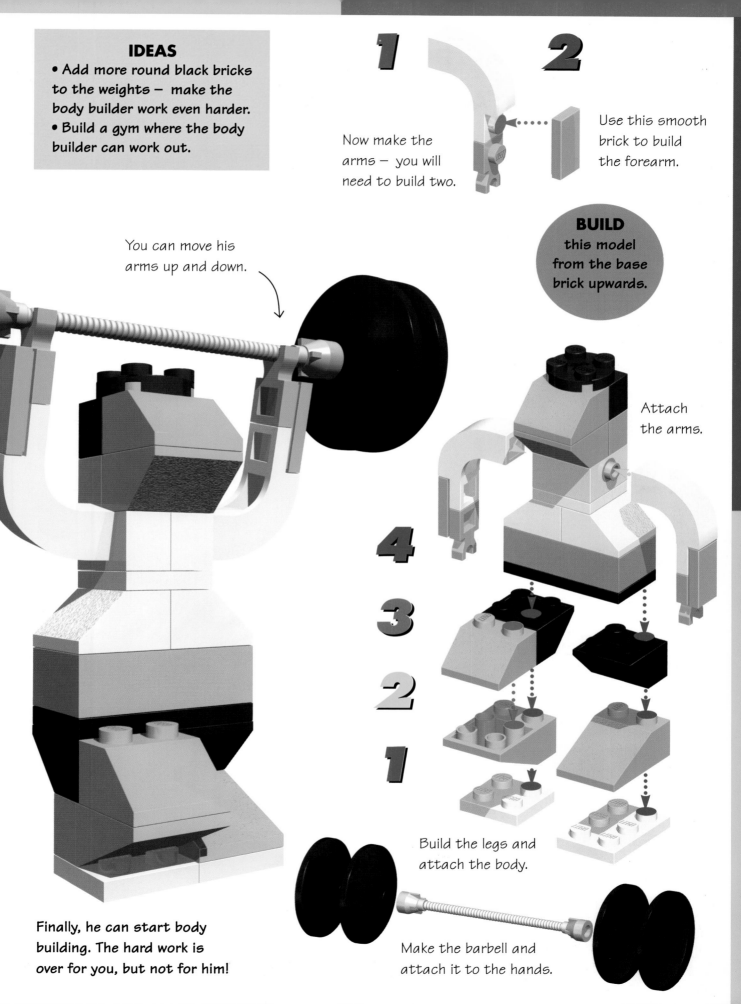

IDEAS
• Add more round black bricks to the weights — make the body builder work even harder.
• Build a gym where the body builder can work out.

1

Now make the arms — you will need to build two.

2

Use this smooth brick to build the forearm.

You can move his arms up and down.

BUILD this model from the base brick upwards.

Attach the arms.

4

3

2

1

Build the legs and attach the body.

Finally, he can start body building. The hard work is over for you, but not for him!

Make the barbell and attach it to the hands.

ROLLER SKATER

This roller skater is learning to balance on his skates, but he's still a bit wobbly.

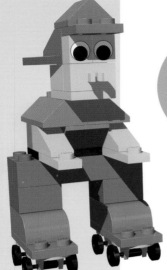

YOU WILL NEED

1 each of these pieces

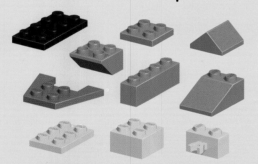

2 each of these pieces

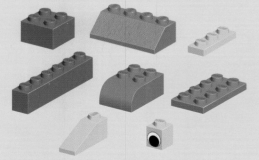

4 each of these pieces

BUILD this model from the base brick upwards.

If you don't have these bricks for the eyes, use plain bricks instead.

Follow each step carefully.

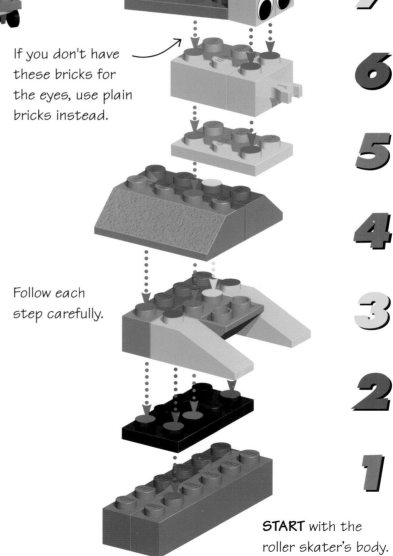

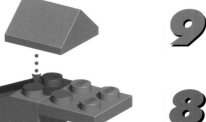

9

8

7

6

5

4

3

2

1

START with the roller skater's body.

There are **34** bricks in this roller skater model.

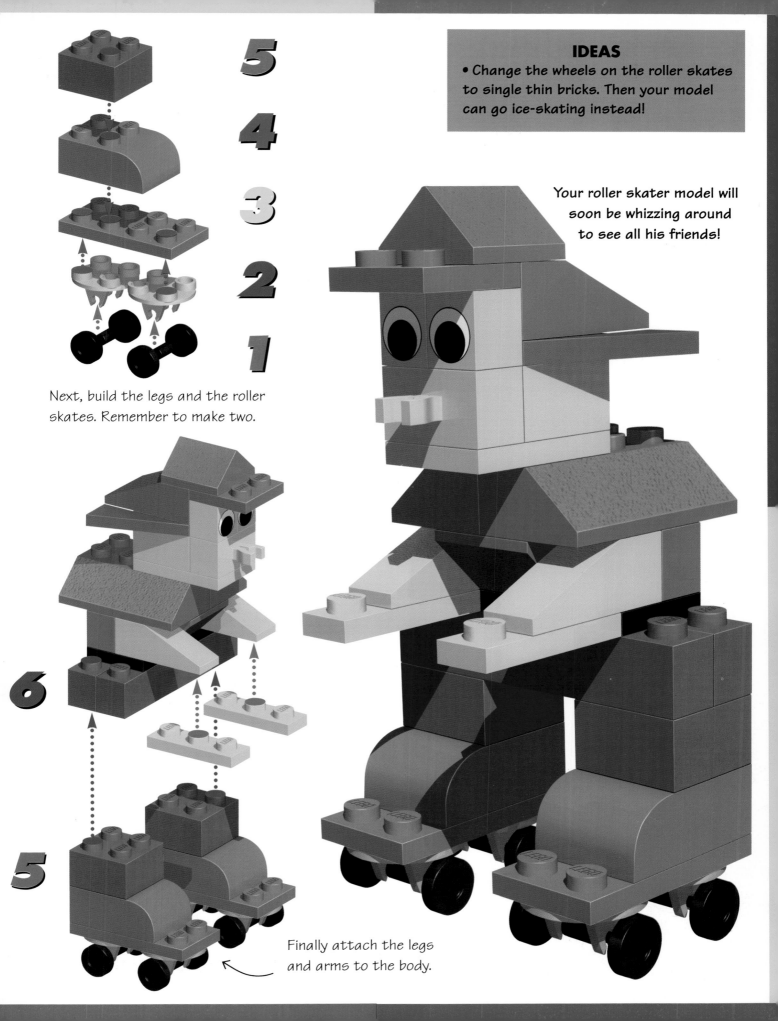

5

4

3

2

1

Next, build the legs and the roller skates. Remember to make two.

IDEAS
• Change the wheels on the roller skates to single thin bricks. Then your model can go ice-skating instead!

Your roller skater model will soon be whizzing around to see all his friends!

6

5

Finally attach the legs and arms to the body.

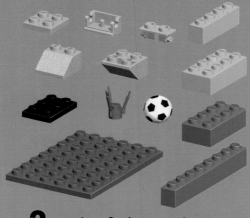

FOOTBALLER

This keen footballer dazzles his fans with his fancy footwork on the football pitch.

YOU WILL NEED

1 each of these pieces

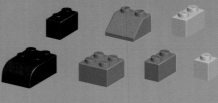

2 each of these pieces

8 of this piece

8

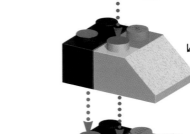
7

This is the face. You could use "eye" bricks if you have them!

6

5

BUILD this model from the base brick upwards.

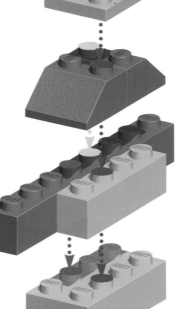
4

The arms will attach to this brick later.

3

2

1

START with the footballer's body.

There are **35** bricks in this footballer model.

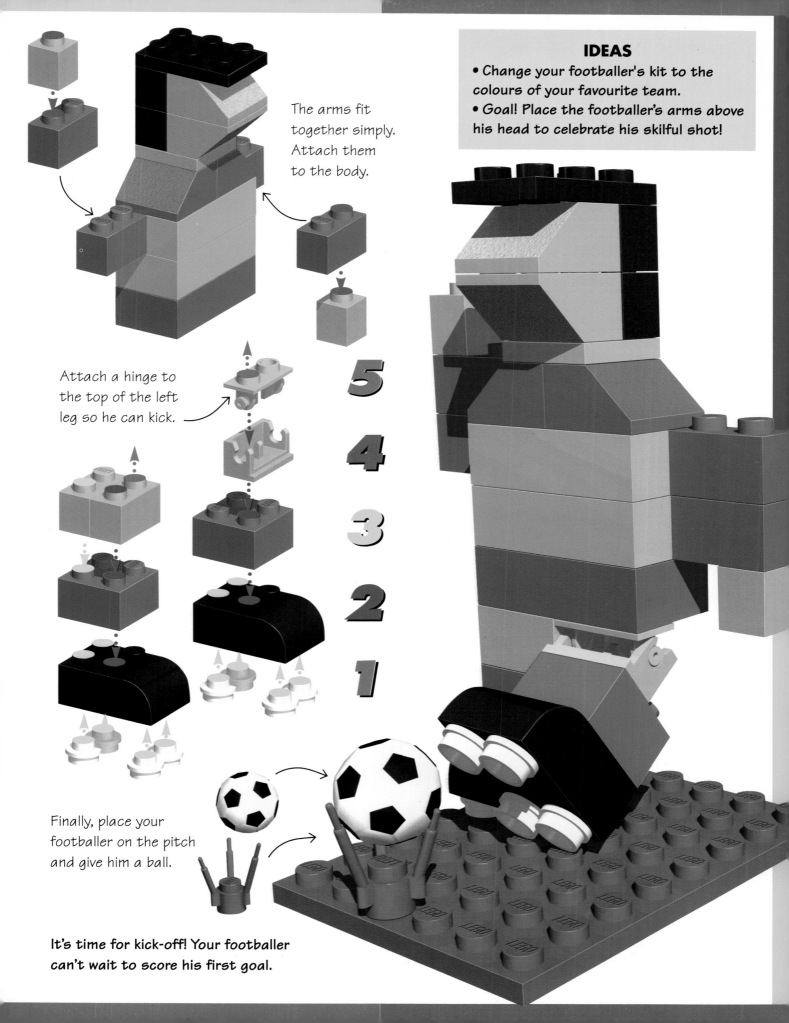

The arms fit together simply. Attach them to the body.

IDEAS
• Change your footballer's kit to the colours of your favourite team.
• Goal! Place the footballer's arms above his head to celebrate his skilful shot!

Attach a hinge to the top of the left leg so he can kick.

5

4

3

2

1

Finally, place your footballer on the pitch and give him a ball.

It's time for kick-off! Your footballer can't wait to score his first goal.

GOLFER

This golfer swings his club, hoping to score a hole in one.

BUILD
this model from the base brick upwards.

YOU WILL NEED

1 each of these pieces

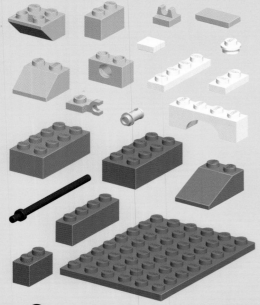

2 each of these pieces

4 of this piece

9

8

7

6

Now build the shoulders and the head.

5

4

Don't forget to add these two bricks. The golf club will attach here later.

3

2

START with the golfer's body.

1

There are **36** bricks in this golfer model.

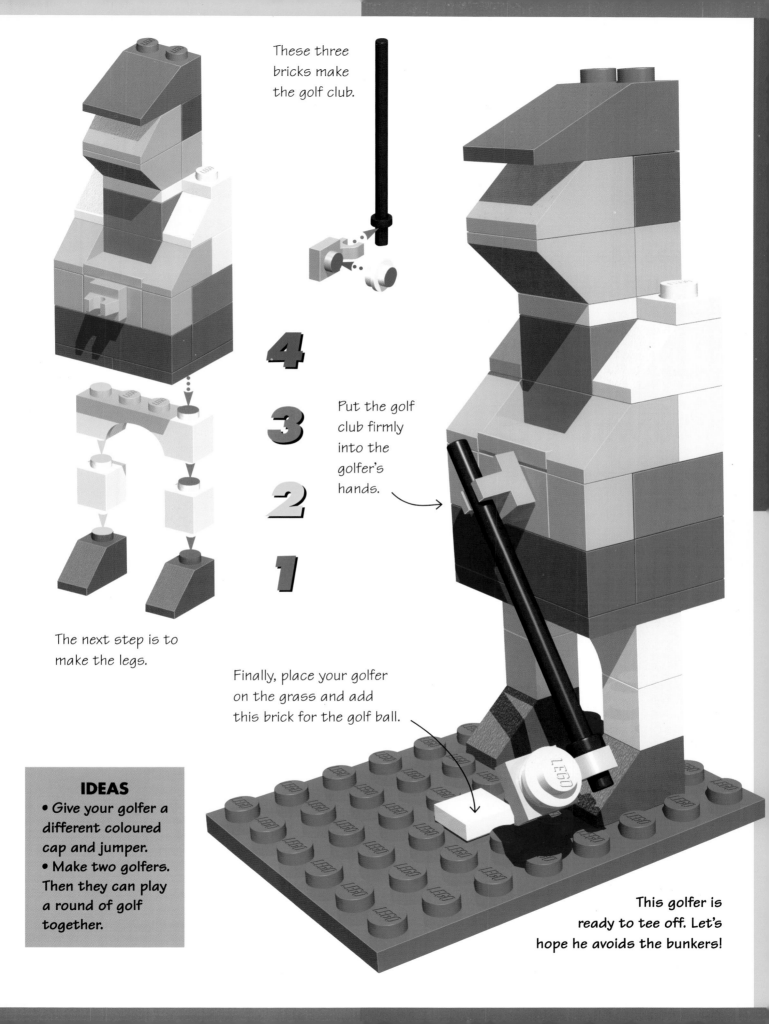

These three bricks make the golf club.

The next step is to make the legs.

4
3
2
1

Put the golf club firmly into the golfer's hands.

Finally, place your golfer on the grass and add this brick for the golf ball.

IDEAS
• Give your golfer a different coloured cap and jumper.
• Make two golfers. Then they can play a round of golf together.

This golfer is ready to tee off. Let's hope he avoids the bunkers!

SKATEBOARDER

Watch this skateboarder zip past! He is the fastest kid in town!

YOU WILL NEED

1 each of these pieces

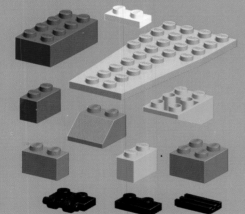

2 each of these pieces

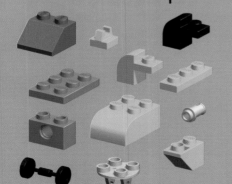

BUILD this model from the base brick upwards.

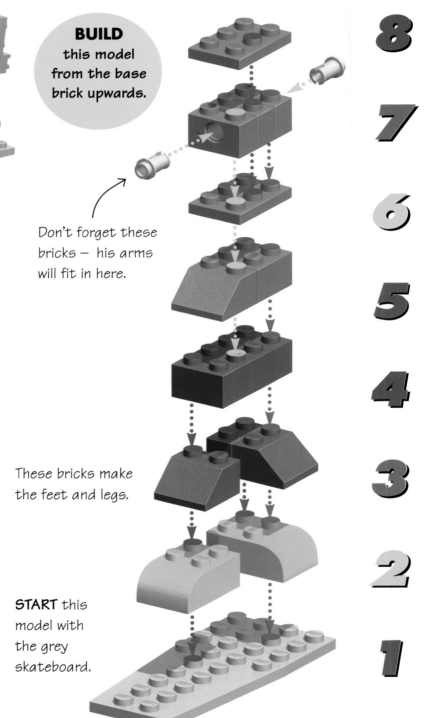

8

7

Don't forget these bricks — his arms will fit in here.

6

5

4

These bricks make the feet and legs.

3

2

START this model with the grey skateboard.

1

There are **36** bricks in this skateboarder model.

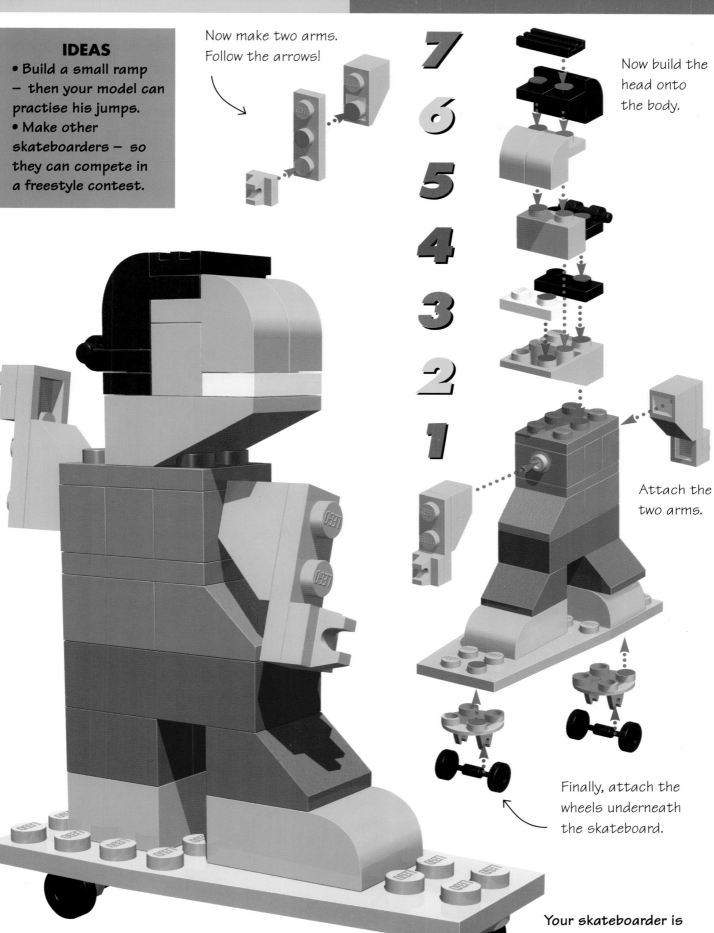

IDEAS
- Build a small ramp — then your model can practise his jumps.
- Make other skateboarders — so they can compete in a freestyle contest.

Now make two arms. Follow the arrows!

7

6

5

4

3

2

1

Now build the head onto the body.

Attach the two arms.

Finally, attach the wheels underneath the skateboard.

Your skateboarder is ready to roll — how many tricks can he do?

DRUMMER

Y ou can't miss this drummer when he marches down the street, banging his cymbal and drum.

YOU WILL NEED

1 each of these pieces

2 each of these pieces

These bricks make the right arm.

6
5
4
3
2
1

Now build the drum and cymbal.

7
6
5
4
3
2
1

This brick is hidden here. The arm will attach here later.

BUILD
this model from the base brick upwards.

START with the drummer's body.

There are **39** bricks in this drummer model.

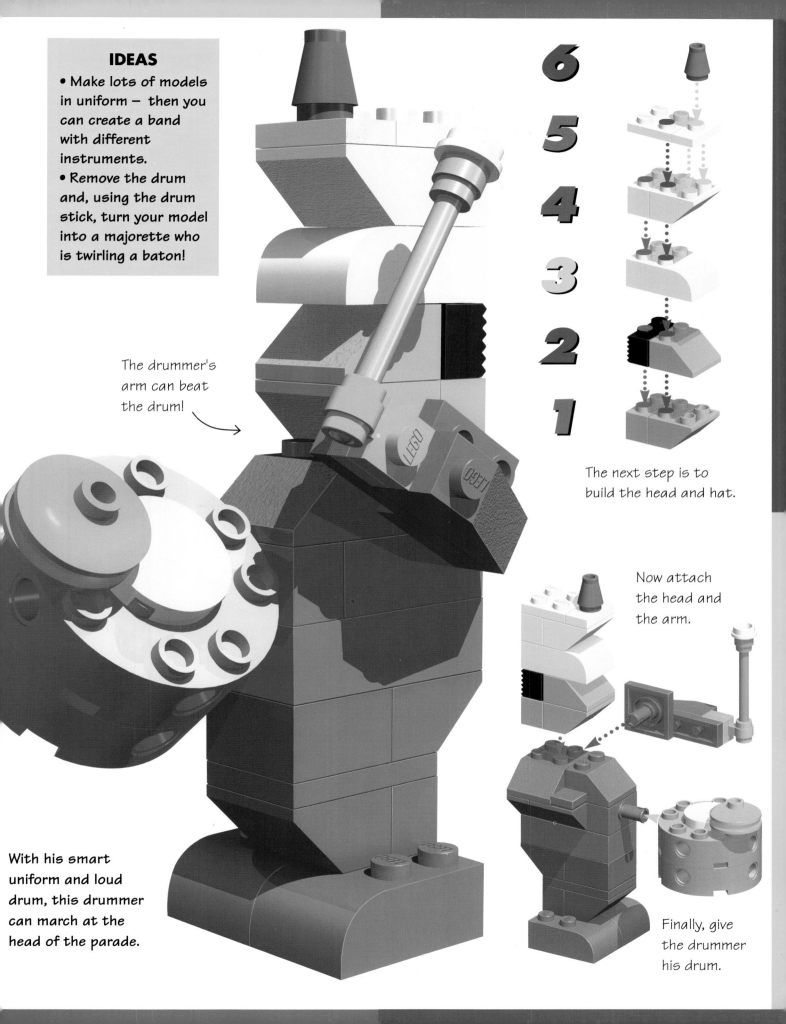

IDEAS
• Make lots of models in uniform – then you can create a band with different instruments.
• Remove the drum and, using the drum stick, turn your model into a majorette who is twirling a baton!

The drummer's arm can beat the drum!

6
5
4
3
2
1

The next step is to build the head and hat.

Now attach the head and the arm.

With his smart uniform and loud drum, this drummer can march at the head of the parade.

Finally, give the drummer his drum.

CAMERAMAN

This cameraman loves to capture his friends on video!

YOU WILL NEED

1 each of these pieces

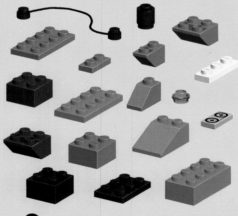

2 each of these pieces

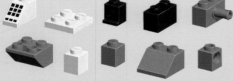

4 of this piece

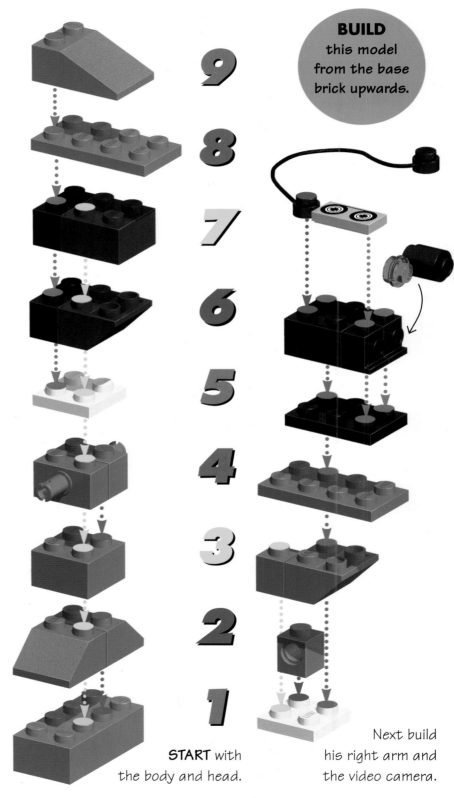

BUILD this model from the base brick upwards.

9

8

7

6

5

4

3

2

1

START with the body and head.

Next build his right arm and the video camera.

There are **42** bricks in this cameraman model.

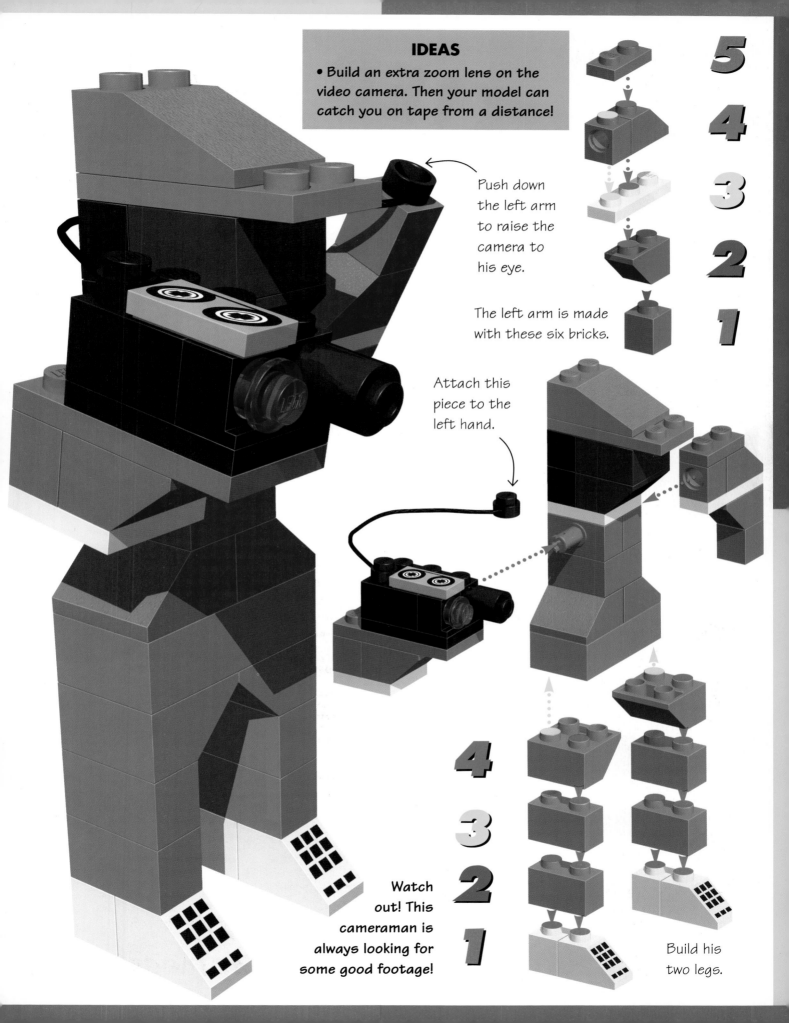

5 4 3 2 1

IDEAS

• Build an extra zoom lens on the video camera. Then your model can catch you on tape from a distance!

Push down the left arm to raise the camera to his eye.

The left arm is made with these six bricks.

Attach this piece to the left hand.

Watch out! This cameraman is always looking for some good footage!

4 3 2 1

Build his two legs.

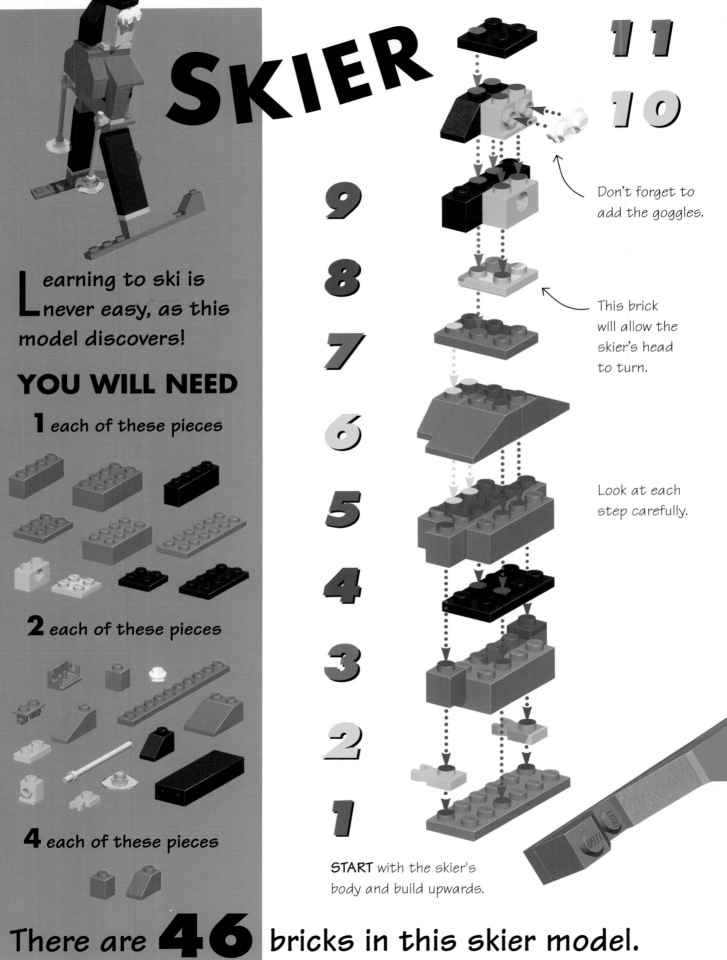

SKIER

Learning to ski is never easy, as this model discovers!

YOU WILL NEED

1 each of these pieces

2 each of these pieces

4 each of these pieces

11

10

Don't forget to add the goggles.

9

8

This brick will allow the skier's head to turn.

7

6

Look at each step carefully.

5

4

3

2

1

START with the skier's body and build upwards.

There are **46** bricks in this skier model.

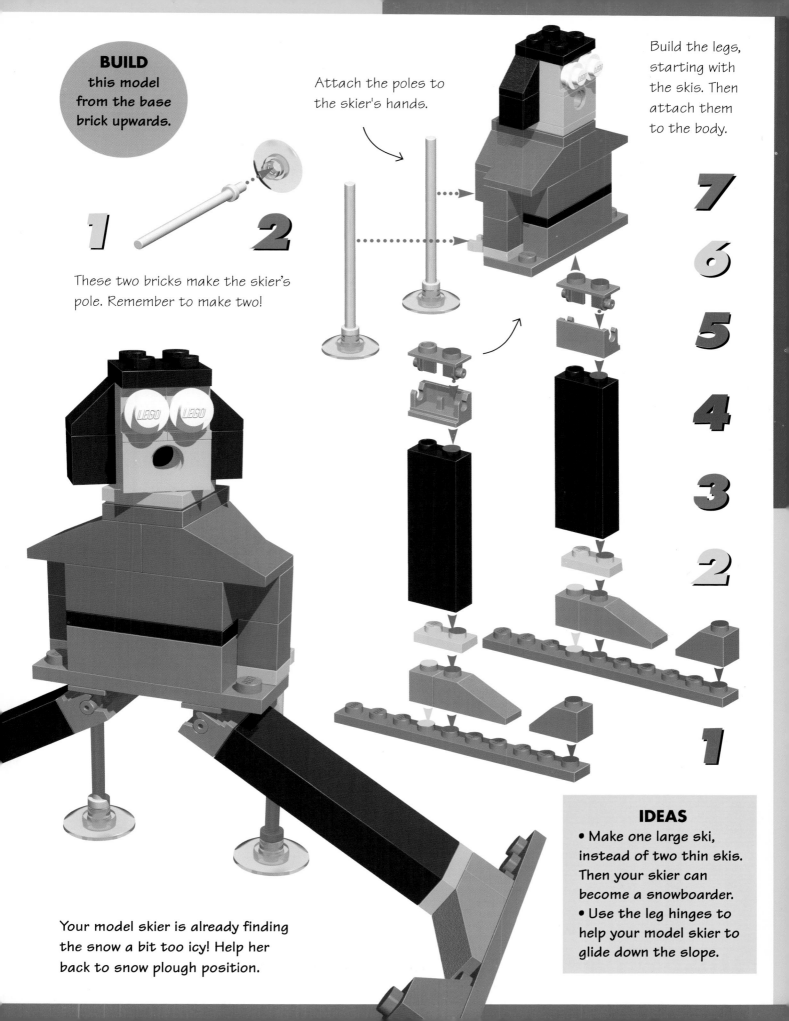

BUILD this model from the base brick upwards.

Attach the poles to the skier's hands.

Build the legs, starting with the skis. Then attach them to the body.

1

2

These two bricks make the skier's pole. Remember to make two!

7

6

5

4

3

2

1

Your model skier is already finding the snow a bit too icy! Help her back to snow plough position.

IDEAS
• Make one large ski, instead of two thin skis. Then your skier can become a snowboarder.
• Use the leg hinges to help your model skier to glide down the slope.

W**ith
one**
swing, the
baseball
goes flying
– this player
sure can
hit hard!

YOU WILL NEED

1 *each of these pieces*

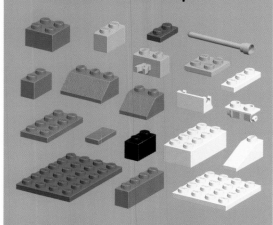

2 *each of these pieces*

3 *each of these pieces*

6 *of this piece*

8 *of this piece*

There are **50** bricks in this baseball player model.

BASEBALL

BUILD
this model
from the base
brick upwards.

This brick will enable
the baseball player's
head to turn. If you
do not have this
brick, use a plain
yellow brick instead.

Look carefully
at each step
before placing
your bricks.

START with
the baseball
player's body.

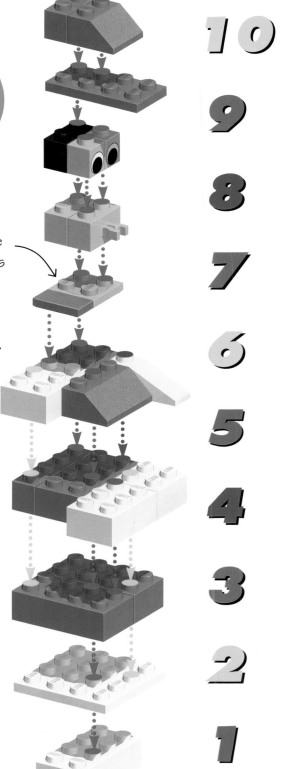

10
9
8
7
6
5
4
3
2
1

PLAYER

The next step is to make the bat.

Now attach the bat onto the hand as shown.

Finally, build the legs onto the small patch of grass.

6
5
4
3
2
1

Batter up! This baseball player is ready to hit another home run.

IDEAS
• Make two teams of baseball players and a baseball diamond on which to play.

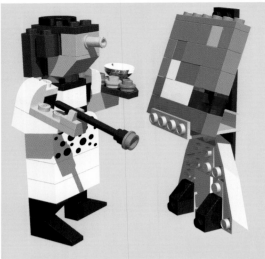

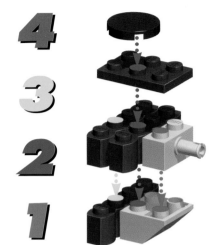

ARTIST

IDEAS
• Create your own painting on the easel. There are so many things this artist can draw!
• Change the artist's clothes — it is easy to spill paint on an overall!

This artist loves creating pictures with her palette of colourful paints.

YOU WILL NEED

1 each of these pieces

2 each of these pieces

3 each of these pieces

4
3
2
1

START with the head.

7
6
5
4
3
2
1

Now build the artist's body.

There are **54** bricks in this artist model.

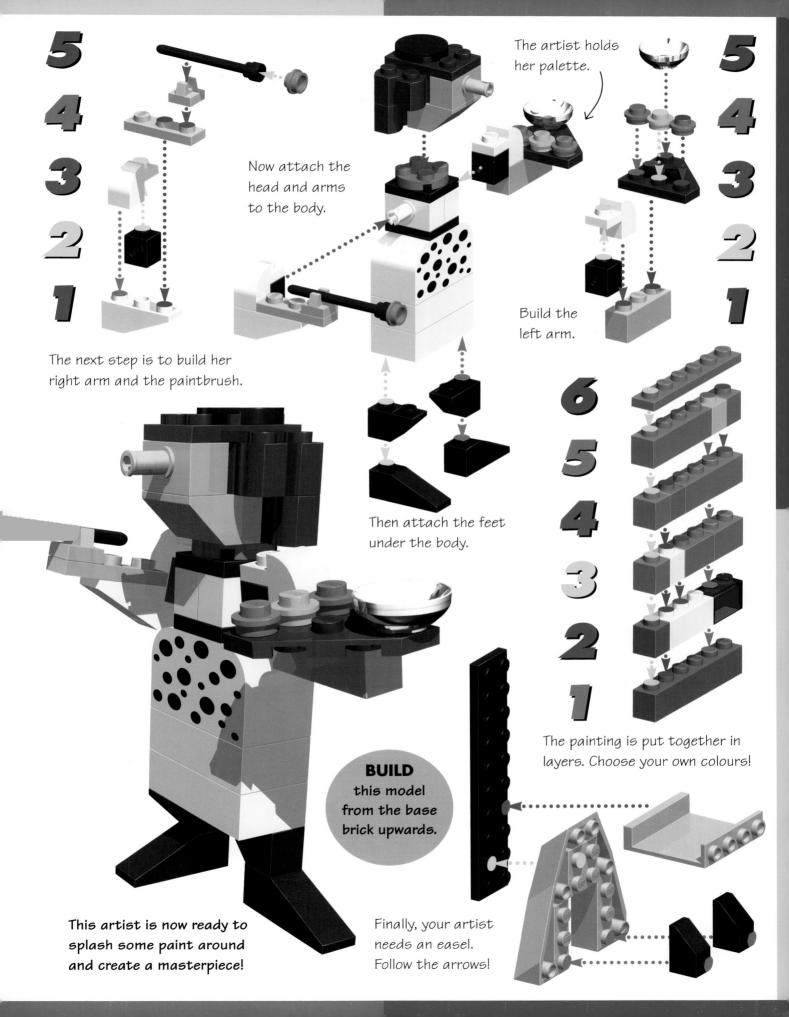

5
4
3
2
1

The next step is to build her right arm and the paintbrush.

Now attach the head and arms to the body.

The artist holds her palette.

5
4
3
2
1

Build the left arm.

6
5
4
3
2
1

Then attach the feet under the body.

The painting is put together in layers. Choose your own colours!

This artist is now ready to splash some paint around and create a masterpiece!

BUILD this model from the base brick upwards.

Finally, your artist needs an easel. Follow the arrows!

BREAK DANCER

This break dancer just loves to show off his moves to his friends!

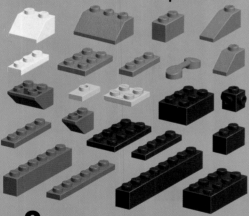

YOU WILL NEED

1 each of these pieces

2 each of these pieces

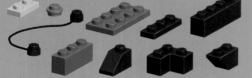

3 of this piece

4 of this piece

7 of this piece

There are **57** bricks in this break dancer model.

11
10
These bricks make the shades — an essential item for this cool kid!

9

8

7

6

5

4
The personal stereo will attach here later.

3

2

1

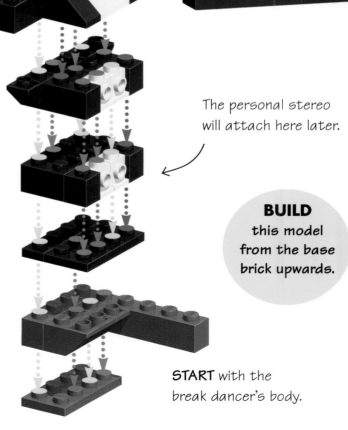

BUILD this model from the base brick upwards.

START with the break dancer's body.

IDEAS
• Turn this model upside down and help him complete a head spin!
• Make a group of break dancers and then they can have a competion. This model always likes a new challenge!

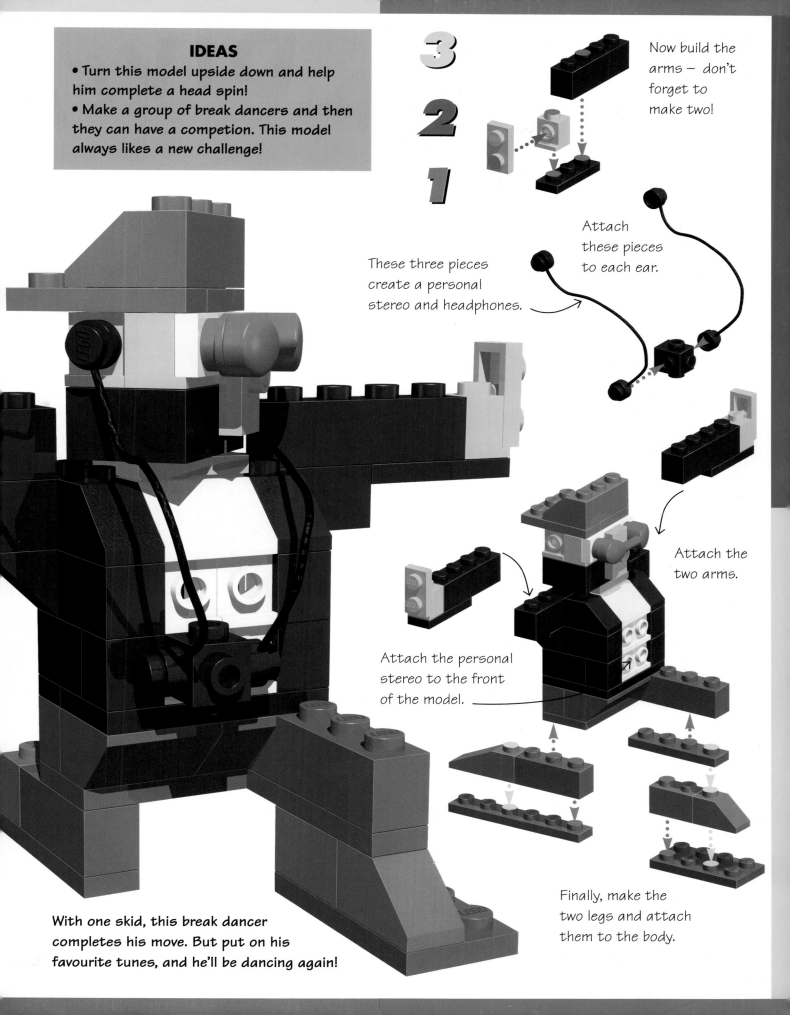

3
2
1

Now build the arms – don't forget to make two!

These three pieces create a personal stereo and headphones.

Attach these pieces to each ear.

Attach the two arms.

Attach the personal stereo to the front of the model.

Finally, make the two legs and attach them to the body.

With one skid, this break dancer completes his move. But put on his favourite tunes, and he'll be dancing again!

SCUBA DIVER

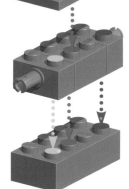

This diver likes to explore the depths of the ocean.

YOU WILL NEED

1 each of these pieces

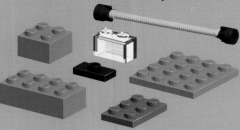

2 each of these pieces

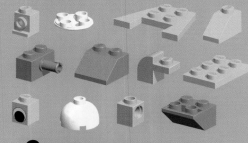

3 each of these pieces

4 each of these pieces

5 of this piece

9

8

7

6

5

4

3

2

1

Follow the black arrows to attach this tube.

This brick will be the diver's mask.

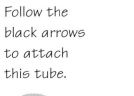

Make the diver's breathing apparatus.

BUILD this model from the base brick upwards.

START with the diver's body.

There are **57** bricks in this scuba diver model.

3

2

1

These bricks will create the oxygen tanks. Make two of these.

Make two of these arms — they will fit onto the body later.

Attach the two cylinders under the blue brick.

Now attach the two arms.

6

5

Finally make the legs. Don't forget the flippers!

4

3

2

1

At last! Now your diver can plunge into deep waters to see the coral reefs.

IDEAS

• Build an underwater world with sharks and fish for your diver to find!

• Remove the diver's mask and tanks and give him a board — he will become a bodyboarder looking for the perfect wave!

See if you can build this guitarist. He is crazy about his music!

YOU WILL NEED

1 each of these pieces

2 each of these pieces

3 of this piece

4 each of these pieces

8 of this piece

ROCK STAR

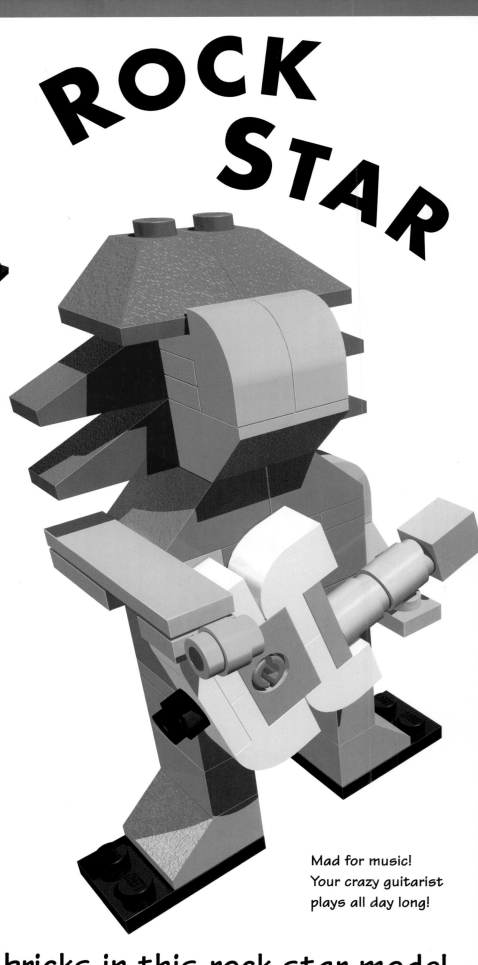

Mad for music! Your crazy guitarist plays all day long!

There are **66** bricks in this rock star model.

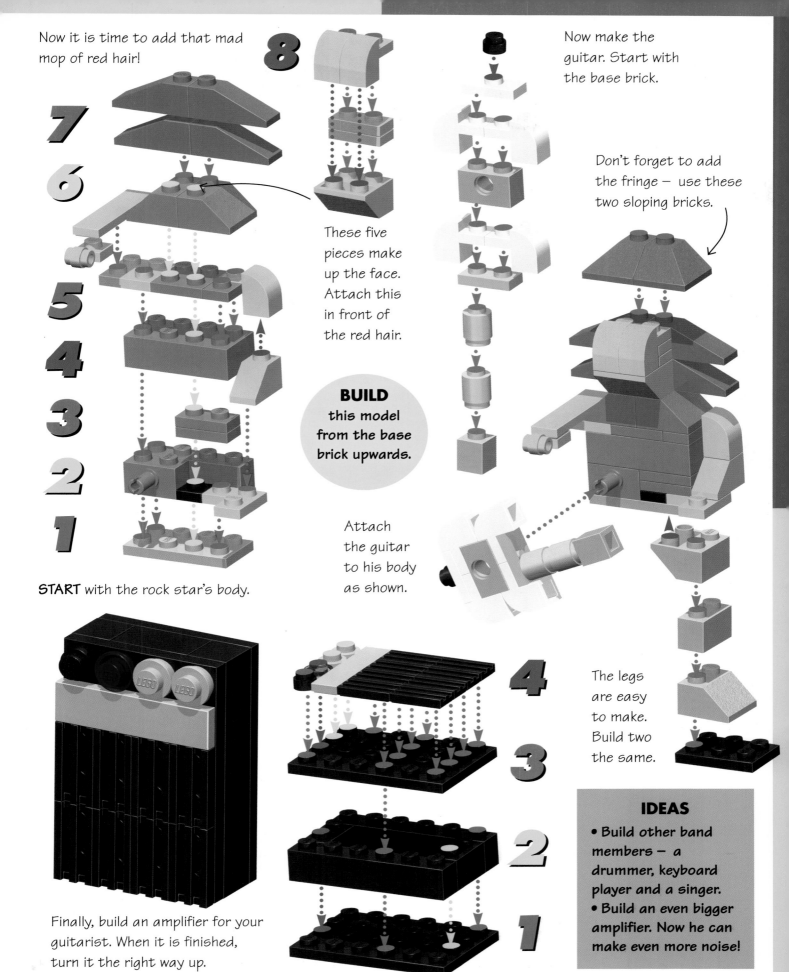

Now it is time to add that mad mop of red hair!

7

6

Now make the guitar. Start with the base brick.

8

Don't forget to add the fringe — use these two sloping bricks.

5

4

These five pieces make up the face. Attach this in front of the red hair.

3

BUILD this model from the base brick upwards.

2

1

Attach the guitar to his body as shown.

START with the rock star's body.

The legs are easy to make. Build two the same.

4

3

2

1

Finally, build an amplifier for your guitarist. When it is finished, turn it the right way up.

IDEAS

• Build other band members — a drummer, keyboard player and a singer.
• Build an even bigger amplifier. Now he can make even more noise!

GOALKEEPER

This ice hockey goalkeeper has to keep his wits about him to save the fast pucks.

YOU WILL NEED

1 each of these pieces

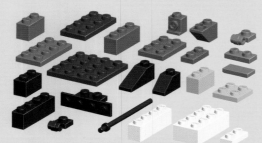

2 each of these pieces

3 each of these pieces

4 of this piece

7 of this piece

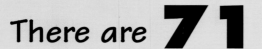

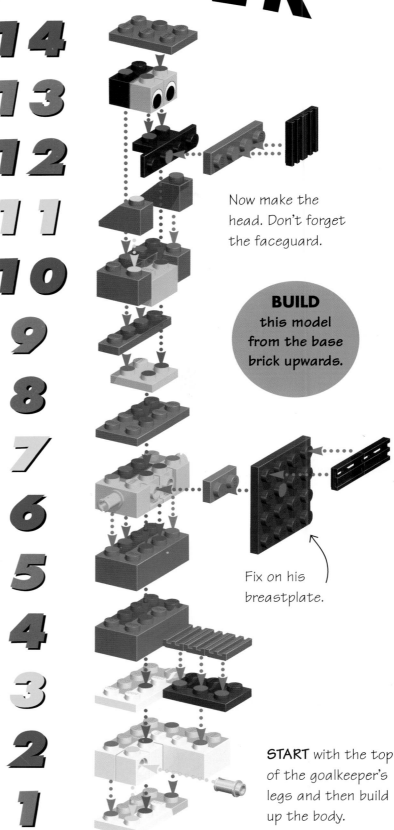

Now make the head. Don't forget the faceguard.

BUILD this model from the base brick upwards.

Fix on his breastplate.

START with the top of the goalkeeper's legs and then build up the body.

There are **71** bricks in this goalkeeper model.

The next step is to build his arms.

4
3
2
1

5

Join the two arms to the body, as shown.

Remember to add the shin pads!

6

7

These bricks make the lower legs.

Give your goalkeeper his hockey stick.

IDEAS
• Build a goal. Then your model can practise his saves.

The hockey stick fits together simply.

With all his padding on, this model is ready to stop the whizzing puck!

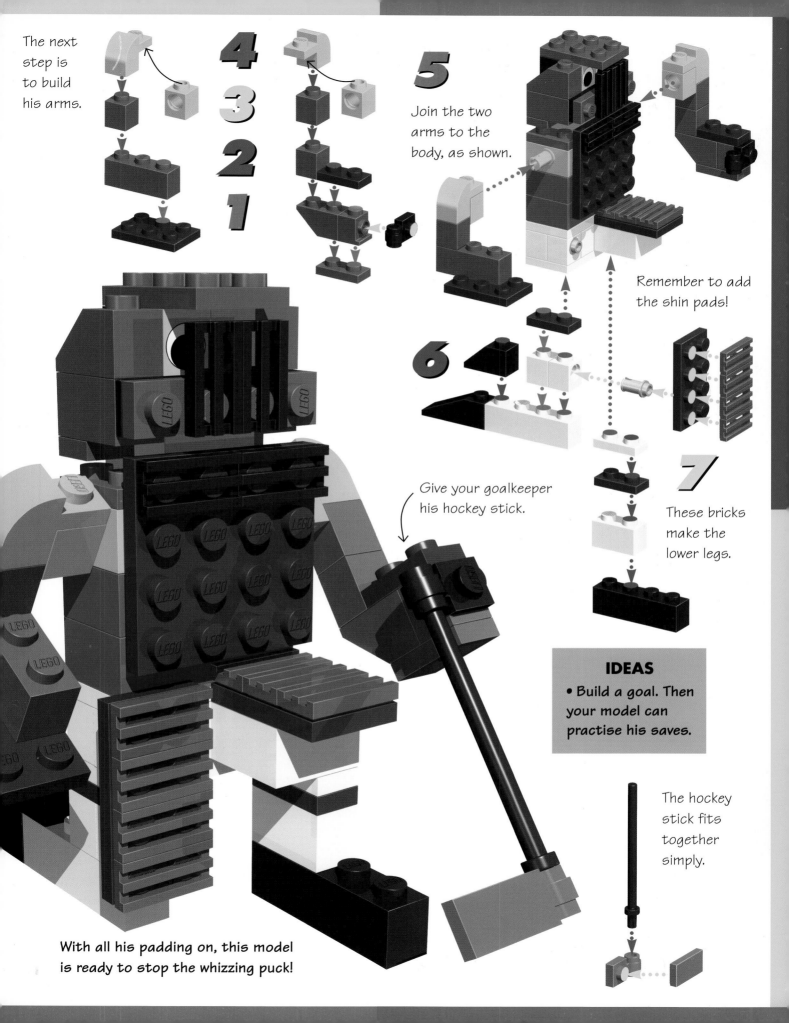

LEGO basic

To find out how you can purchase LEGO toys on-line visit:

www.legoworldshop.com

THE LEGO BOOK RANGE ALSO INCLUDES:

LEGO MODELLERS:
Build Amazing Animals

PUZZLE STORYBOOKS:
The Lost Temple
Rock Raiders
Castle Mystery
The Curse of the Mummy

ROAD MAZE GAME BOOKS:
Spy Catcher
Jewel Thief
Treasure Smuggler
Gold Robber

ALSO LOOK FOR:
The Ultimate LEGO Book

DK

www.dk.com

Text copyright © 1999 LEGO Group
Illustrations © 1999 LEGO Group
Art Editor: Goldberry Broad
Project Editor: Rebecca Smith
Managing Art Editor: Cathy Tincknell
Managing Editor: Joanna Devereux
DTP Designer: Jill Bunyan
Production: Steve Lang

First published in Great Britain in 1999
by Dorling Kindersley Limited, 9 Henrietta Street, London, WC2E 8PS

2 4 6 8 10 9 7 5 3 1

A CIP catalogue record for this book is available from the British Library.

ISBN 0-7513-6203-4

Colour reproduction by Dot Gradations
Printed and bound in Italy by L.E.G.O.

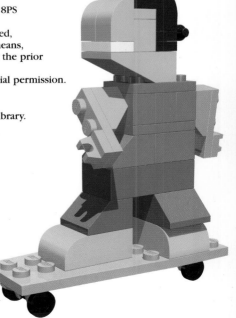